C000128741

50 Prayers for Your Children and Generations to Come

Bisi Oladipupo

Springs of Life Publishing

Copyright © 2024 by Bisi Oladipupo

Springs of life publishing

ISBN: 978-1-915269-39-3 (ePub e-book)

ISBN: 978-1-915269-38-6 (paperback)

All Rights Reserved.

No part of this book may be used or reproduced by any means, graphic, electronic, or mechanical, including photocopying, recording, taping, or by any information storage retrieval system without the written permission of the publisher except in the case of brief quotations embodied in critical articles and reviews.

Printed in the United Kingdom

Unless otherwise indicated, scripture quotations are taken from the New King James Version.

Scripture taken from the New King James Version®. Copyright © 1982 by Thomas Nelson. Used by permission. All rights reserved.

Scripture quotations from The Authorized (King James) Version. Rights in the Authorized Version in the United Kingdom are vested in the Crown. Reproduced by permission of the Crown's patentee, Cambridge University Press.

Scripture quotations marked (AMP) are taken from the Amplified Bible, Copyright © 2015 by The Lockman Foundation. Used by permission.

CONTENTS

To Jesus Christ my Lord and saviour; to Him alone that laid down His life that l might have life eternal. To Him that lead captivity captive and gave gifts unto men (Ephesians 4; 8). One of those gifts is writing!

Bisi Oladipupo

INTRODUCTION

S o, why do we need to pray?

We need to pray because the scriptures tell us to.

The Lord knows what we need, but we still need to ask.

The Bible tells us that we have not because we do not ask (James 4:2).

There is a reason the scriptures tell us to ask:

"Until now you have asked nothing in My name. Ask, and you will receive, that your joy may be full" (John 16:24).

The Lord wants us to have full joy regarding our children and future generations.

Our effective prayers avail much and are powerful (James 5:16).

So, we can see that we do have to pray. For prayer to be effective, it must be according to the Word of God.

The prayers in this book are based on God's Word and inspired by the Holy Spirit, our helper.

Remember that some things take time. We must allow God to work when we pray, but one thing is certain: your effective prayers do prevail.

God is on our side. He wants to help and work on our behalf, and He is just waiting for our prayers.

But can we also pray for our future generations?

Yes, we can.

Jesus set an example for us:

"*I do not pray for these alone, but also for those who [j] will believe in Me through their word*" (John 17:20).

We are the future generation of believers in Christ that Jesus Christ prayed for during His earthly ministry. Therefore, we can pray for our generations to come.

The prayer of the upright is His delight (Proverbs 15:8).

Our prayers are important.

We can see how effective Elijah's prayer was from Scripture. The Bible tells us that Elijah was a man just like us:

"Elijah was a man with a nature like ours, and he prayed earnestly that it would not rain; and it did not rain on the land for three years and six months. And he prayed again, and the heaven gave rain, and the earth produced its fruit" (James 5:17-18).

We are now a royal priesthood (1 Peter 2:9), and we can stand in the gap for our children and generations to come.

The focal point of the prayers in this book is for your children to fulfil their God-ordained destiny in Christ and be a good representation of the person of Christ.

You will find several prayers that will help you lay up a legacy in the spirit for your children and generations to come.

1

LORD, DIRECT THEIR HEARTS INTO THE LOVE OF GOD

In the Book of Thessalonians, Paul prayed: *"And the Lord direct your hearts into the love of God, and into the patient waiting for Christ"* (2 Thessalonians 3:5).

Father God, I pray that you will direct my children's hearts into the love of God and patient waiting of Christ in Jesus' name.

I pray that my children's hearts will be so rooted in the love of God for them that their first priority will be for you and your kingdom. I also pray that as their hearts are directed towards the patient waiting of Christ, this will affect their conduct, and they will live upright lives to your glory in Jesus' name. Amen.

2

DECLARE THAT YOUR FUTURE GENERATIONS ARE BLESSED

---

*B**lessed is the man who fears the Lord, Who delights greatly in His commandments.*

His descendants will be mighty on earth; The generation of the upright will be blessed (Psalm 112:1-2).

Father, I thank you that I can claim this scripture for my generation. I align myself with the conditions of this promise.

My descendants will be mighty upon the earth. They will walk with you and reign in this life through Christ Jesus (Romans 5:17).

My generation will be blessed. Blessed going out, blessed coming in, blessed in the fruit of their body, and walking in the blessing of the Lord in Jesus' name. Amen.

3

STAND PERFECT AND COMPLETE IN ALL THE WILL OF GOD FOR THEIR LIVES

F ather, I pray that all my children will stand perfect and complete in all the will of God for their lives in Jesus' name.

The scriptures say in the Book of Colossians 4:12: "*Epaphras, who is one of you, a bondservant of Christ, greets you, always laboring fervently for you in prayers, that you may stand perfect and [c]complete in all the will of God*".

I labour in the place of prayer for my children in Jesus' name. They will stand perfect and complete in all the will of God for their lives.

4

CALL YOUR FUTURE GENERATIONS INTO THE KINGDOM OF GOD

F ather, I call my generations into the kingdom of God in
Jesus' name. Your word says in 1 Timothy 2:4, *"Who will
have all men to be saved, and to come unto the knowledge of the
truth"*.

All men include my generation; therefore, I call them into the
kingdom of God in Jesus' name. None of them will miss heaven
in Jesus' name.

Thank you for your angels already at work, including those not
yet born.

5

CREATED TO BRING GOD PLEASURE

F ather, according to Revelation 4:11, you created all things for your pleasure.

"Thou art worthy, O Lord, to receive glory and honour and power: for thou hast created all things, and for thy pleasure they are and were created".

Father, I agree with your word that my children will bring you pleasure. They will fulfil their destinies and live godly lives in Jesus' name. Amen.

6

CUT OFF UNGODLY INFLUENCES OVER THEIR LIVES

F ather, your word says in the Book of Matthew 18:18:

"Assuredly, I say to you, whatever you bind on earth will be bound in heaven, and whatever you loose on earth will be loosed in heaven".

I take my authority in the name of the Lord Jesus Christ, and I cut off all ungodly influences over my children's lives in Jesus' name.

Lord, I declare that you are a wall of fire around my children (Zechariah 2:5), shielding them from all ungodly influences in Jesus' name.

7

THEIR HEARTS TO BE ESTABLISHED UNBLAMEABLE IN HOLINESS

F ather, your word says in the Book of 1 Thessalonians 3:13:

"To the end he may stablish your hearts unblameable in holiness before God, even our Father, at the coming of our Lord Jesus Christ with all his saints".

Father, l pray that my children's hearts will be established unblameable in holiness, in Jesus' name. I pray that my children will pay attention to your dealings in their hearts and live from a pure heart in your sight, in Jesus' name.

8

PRESERVE MY CHILDREN UNTO YOUR HEAVENLY KINGDOM

Father, your word says in 2 Timothy 4:18:

"And the Lord shall deliver me from every evil work, and will preserve me unto his heavenly kingdom: to whom be glory for ever and ever. Amen".

Lord, l ask that you deliver my children from every evil work and preserve them unto your heavenly kingdom in Jesus' name.

My children will make heaven their final home in Jesus' name.

Thank you for your keeping and preserving power in Jesus' name.

9

THERE SHALL BE NO BARRENNESS IN MY GENERATIONS TO COME

F ather, your word says in the Book of Psalms 127:3-4:s

"Behold, children are a heritage from the Lord, The fruit of the womb is a reward. Like arrows in the hand of a warrior, So are the children of one's youth".

I declare that my future generations are fruitful in Jesus' name. I refuse barrenness in my generations to come in Jesus' name.

My grandchildren, great-grandchildren, and those to come will be mighty arrows in the hand of the Lord, in Jesus' name.

GRACE TO SERVE THE LORD ACCEPTABLY

F ather, your word says in the Book of Hebrews 12:28-29:

"Therefore, since we are receiving a kingdom which cannot be shaken, let us have grace, by which we [1] may serve God acceptably with reverence and godly fear. 29 For our God is a consuming fire".

Father, your word also says that we should come boldly unto the throne of grace to obtain mercy and find grace to help in times of need (Hebrews 4:16).

Lord, l ask that you grant my children grace so they may serve you acceptably with reference and godly fear in Jesus' name. Amen.

11

ABOUND IN HOPE

F ather, your word says in the Book of Romans 15:13:

"Now may the God of hope fill you with all joy and peace in believing, that you may abound in hope by the power of the Holy Spirit".

Father, l pray that whatever my children go through in life, they will abound in hope through the power of the Holy Spirit in Jesus' name. Amen.

12

FERVENT IN SPIRIT, SERVING THE LORD

F ather, your will is for everyone to be fervent in spirit in serving you.

"not lagging in diligence, fervent in spirit, serving the Lord" (Romans 12:11). In the Book of Revelation 3:13-15, you prefer your people to be hot.

Therefore, l call my children fervent in spirit, serving the Lord in Jesus' name. Amen.

My children will have their priorities right regarding spiritual matters, causing them to discern that making you their priority is only wisdom in Jesus' name. Amen.

13

A SOUND MIND

F ather, your word says in the Book of First Timothy 1:7:

"For God has not given us a spirit of fear, but of power and of love and of a sound mind" (1 Timothy 1:7).

I agree with your word, and I declare that all my children have a sound mind in Jesus' name.

This sound mind affects their belief system, and with the help of the Holy Spirit, they will rightly divide the word of truth in Jesus' name. Amen.

They will walk in sound faith, doctrine, and a truthful perspective of who you really are in Jesus' name. Amen.

14

DELIVER THEM FROM EVERY EVIL WORK

F ather, the Lord, during His earthly ministry, when teaching His disciples to pray, said, *"and deliver us from evil"* (Matthew 6:13).

When Jesus was praying for His disciples in the book of John, He said, *"keep them from the evil one"* (John 17:15).

Lord, l ask that you deliver and keep my children from all forms of evil in Jesus' name. I also take my authority, and l break every plot of the enemy and render them null and void over my children, in Jesus' name.

15

LORD, REVEAL YOUR LOVE TO MY CHILDREN

Heavenly Father, your word is clear in Scripture that knowing your love greatly impacts our walk with you. Your word says in the Book of Ephesians:

"To know the love of Christ which passes knowledge; that you may be filled with all the fullness of God" (Ephesians 3:19).

Paul wrote in the Book of Romans 8:38-39:

"For I am persuaded that neither death nor life, nor angels nor principalities nor powers, nor things present nor things to come, nor height nor depth, nor any other created thing, shall be able to separate us from the love of God which is in Christ Jesus our Lord".

Father, l ask that you reveal your love to my children so they will be persuaded that nothing will separate them from your love for them in Jesus' name.

16

DECLARE PSALM 121 OVER THEM

Father, I declare Psalm 121 over my children in Jesus' name. (Insert their names).

I will lift up my eyes to the hills—From whence comes my help?² My help comes from the Lord, Who made heaven and earth.

³ He will not allow your foot to [a] be moved; He who keeps you will not slumber.⁴ Behold, He who keeps Israel Shall neither slumber nor sleep.

⁵ The Lord is your [b] keeper; The Lord is your shade at your right hand.⁶ The sun shall not strike you by day, Nor the moon by night.

⁷ The Lord shall [c]preserve you from all evil;He shall preserve your soul.⁸ The Lord shall preserve[d] your going out and your coming inFrom this time forth, and even forevermore (Psalm 121:1-8).

17

SPIRITUAL SENSITIVITY SO THEY DO NOT MISS GODLY DIVINE APPOINTMENTS.

Father, your word says in the Book of Ecclesiastes 9:11:

I returned and saw under the sun that—

The race is not to the swift, Nor the battle to the strong, Nor bread to the wise, Nor riches to men of understanding, Nor favor to men of skill; But time and chance happen to them all.

Father, l ask that my children have spiritual sensitivity to discern godly and divine appointments that you bring across their paths in Jesus' name. That they will not miss it due to carelessness or a lack of spiritual discernment. I pray that my children will know how to be led by your Spirit so they can walk in their godly destinies in Jesus' name. Amen.

18

FILL THEM WITH THE KNOWLEDGE OF YOUR WILL

F ather, in Jesus' name, l pray the prayer found in the Book of Colossians for my children:

"Father l pray that my children may be filled with the knowledge of your will in all wisdom and spiritual understanding; that they may walk worthy of the Lord, fully pleasing you, being fruitful in every good work and increasing in the knowledge of God; strengthened with all might, according to you glorious power, for all patience and longsuffering with joy;" (Customised from Colossians 1:9-11).

Father, l thank you that my children will be fruitful in every good work, laying up treasures in heaven. They will be strong in you according to your own might in Jesus' name. Amen.

19

OPEN DOORS MEANT TO BE OPENED AND SHUT THOSE NEEDED TO BE SHUT

Father, your word says in the Book of Revelation 3:7:

"And to the angel of the church in Philadelphia write; These things saith he that is holy, he that is true, he that hath the key of David, he that openeth, and no man shutteth; and shutteth, and no man openeth".

Lord, if there is any door that will lead to disaster in my children's lives, any wrong choice regarding marriage, job, or associations, let those doors be shut in Jesus' name.

Heavenly Father, let only doors that you have a hand in be opened in my children's lives in Jesus' name. My children will marry the right person, associate with the right people in each season of their lives, and make the right decisions according to your will for their lives in Jesus' name.

20

YOUR KINGDOM COME, YOUR WILL BE DONE ON EARTH

F ather, during Jesus' earthly ministry, when His disciples asked Him how to pray, part of the response was,

"Your kingdom come.

Your will be doneOn earth as it is in heaven" (Matthew 6:10).

This is your will for mankind.

Father, I pray that what you desire and your blueprint for my children's destiny will be fulfilled in Jesus' name. Right here on earth in their lives, as it is in heaven in Jesus' name.

Father, l thank you for your angels at work in my children's lives and for arranging circumstances to conform to your will for their lives in Jesus' name. Amen.

21

WISE UNTO SALVATION

Father, I pray that my children will be wise unto their salvation.

Your word says in the 2nd Book of Timothy 3:15: *"And that from a child thou hast known the holy scriptures, which are able to make thee wise unto salvation through faith which is in Christ Jesus"*.

Father, give them a hunger for your word, and as they study your word and give themselves wholly to them, they will take their walk with you seriously in Jesus' name.

Lord, give them a spiritual understanding of their great salvation in Christ, in Jesus' name. Amen.

22

TILL CHRIST BE FORMED IN THEM

F ather, your plan for everyone in Christ is for them to conform to Christ's image (Romans 8:29).

Your word says in the Book of Galatians 4:19: *"My little children, of whom I travail in birth again until Christ be formed in you"*.

Father, l pray that Christ will be formed in my children, that the word of Christ will dwell in them richly, and they will be good representations of the person of Christ in Jesus' name.

23

WALK IN THEIR ORDAINED CAREER PATH

F ather, your word says in the Book of Proverbs 18:16:

"*A man's gift makes room for him, And brings him before great men*".

Father, I pray that my children will walk their ordained career path in Jesus' name. The giftings you have placed in them will be celebrated and developed in Jesus' name.

24

PROCESS THINGS RIGHTLY

F ather, your word says in the Book of Timothy 1:7:

"For God has not given us a spirit of fear, but of power and of love and of a sound mind".

Father, I agree with your word that my children have sound minds in Jesus' name.

When they go through trials in life, they will process things correctly through the lenses of your character and your word in Jesus' name.

My children will not be discouraged or have wrong belief systems in Jesus' name.

Let them have such a revelation of your love and know your ways, which will reflect on how they handle the trials of this life in Jesus' name. Amen.

25

GODLY ASSOCIATIONS

F ather, your word says in the Book of Proverbs 13:20:

He who walks with wise men will be wise, But the companion of fools will be destroyed.

Father, l declare that my children will walk with wise men. They will walk with godly men in Jesus' name.

Father, l ask that you bring godly people with good hearts across my children's path in Jesus' name.

26

MY CHILDREN'S LOVE TO ABOUND AND GROW

F ather, in the Book of Philippians 1:9-11, this prayer is recorded:

"And this I pray, that your love may abound still more and more in knowledge and all discernment, that you may approve the things that are excellent, that you may be sincere and without offense till the day of Christ, being filled with the fruits of righteousness which are by Jesus Christ, to the glory and praise of God".

Heavenly Father, I am now appropriating this prayer for my children.

I pray that my children's love will abound more and more in knowledge and discernment. May they judge and discern things through how much you love them. Father, I pray that as they abound in your love, they will approve excellent things and be sincere and without offence until the day of Christ. They will not be offended because they will rightly discern and judge things and never blame you. The enemy is the god of this world. Your word says, "Blessed is he that is not offended in me" (Matthew 11:6).

I pray that they will be filled with the fruits of righteousness which are in Jesus Christ, in Jesus' name. Amen.

27

SPIRIT OF WISDOM AND KNOWLEDGE IN THE REVELATION OF THE LORD

F ather Paul prayed this prayer in the Book of Ephesians
1:17-21:

*"That the God of our Lord Jesus Christ, the Father of glory, may
give to you the spirit of wisdom and revelation in the knowledge
of Him, the eyes of your [f]understanding being enlightened; that
you may know what is the hope of His calling, what are the riches
of the glory of His inheritance in the saints, and what is the exceeding greatness of His power toward us who believe, according to
the working of His mighty power which He worked in Christ when
He raised Him from the dead and seated Him at His right hand*

in the heavenly places, far above all principality[g] and [h]power
and [I]might and dominion, and every name that is named, not
only in this age but also in that which is to come".

Father, l pray that the God of our Lord Jesus Christ, the Father
of glory, may give unto my children the spirit of wisdom and
revelation in the knowledge of Him, that the eyes of their [f]un-
derstanding be enlightened, and they may know what the hope
of Your calling is. I pray that they know the riches of the glory
of Your inheritance in the saints and the exceeding greatness of
Your power toward them that believe, according to the working
of His mighty power which He worked in Christ when He
raised Him from the dead and seated *Him* at His right hand in
the heavenly *places,* far above all principality and power, might
and dominion, and every name that is named, not only in this
age but also in that which is to come in Jesus' name. Amen.

28

MY DESCENDANTS SHALL BE MIGHTY UPON THE EARTH

Father, your word says in the Book of Psalm 112:1-2:

"Praise the Lord!

Blessed is the man who fears the Lord, Who delights greatly in His commandments.

His descendants will be mighty on earth; The generation of the upright will be blessed".

Heavenly Father, I align myself to the conditions of this promise, and I declare that my descendants will be mighty upon the earth in Jesus' name. They will diligently study your word and know who they are in Christ, in Jesus' name.

They will walk in the God-ordained authority of Christ, in Jesus' name. Amen.

29

GOOD SENSITIVITY TO THE VOICE OF THE LORD

F ather, your word says in the Book of John 10:27:

My sheep hear My voice, and I know them, and they follow Me.

Father, I agree with your word over my children that they will hear your voice in Jesus' name. Lord, I pray that my children will be sensitive to your voice and know when you speak to them clearly in Jesus' name.

I say that they will not hear the voice of a stranger in Jesus' name.

30

MY CHILDREN ARE FOR SIGNS AND WONDERS

F ather, your word says in the Book of Isaiah 8:18:

"Behold, I and the children whom the Lord hath given me are for signs and for wonders in Israel from the Lord of hosts, which dwelleth in mount Zion".

Father, l declare that my children will be for signs and wonders in Jesus' name. They will declare to others who Jesus is. The Lord will work through them mightily, in Jesus' name. My children will follow the Lord dearly as good children, in Jesus' name. They will bring glory to the name of the Lord, in Jesus' name.

31

THAT MY CHILDREN MAY KNOW THE LORD AND THE POWER OF HIS RESURRECTION

Father, in the Book of Philippians 3:10 (KJV), Paul expresses a desire:

"That I may know him, and the power of his resurrection, and the fellowship of his sufferings, being made conformable unto his death".

"And this, so that I may know Him [experientially, becoming more thoroughly acquainted with Him, understanding the remarkable wonders of His Person more completely] and [in that same way experience] the power of His resurrection [which over-

flows and is active in believers], and [that I may share] the fellow-ship of His sufferings, by being continually conformed [inwardly into His likeness even] to His death [dying as He did]" (Philippians 3:10; AMP).

Father, l am praying this prayer for my children:

That they may know you [experientially, becoming more thoroughly acquainted with you, understanding the remarkable wonders of the person of Jesus more completely] and [in that same way experience] the power of His resurrection [which overflows and is active in believers], and [that they may share] the fellowship of His sufferings, by being *continually* conformed [inwardly into His likeness even] to His death [dying as He did], in Jesus' name.

32

Declare Isaiah 11:2–3 Over Them

F ather, your word says in the Book of Isaiah:

"And the spirit of the Lord shall rest upon him, the spirit of wisdom and understanding, the spirit of counsel and might, the spirit of knowledge and of the fear of the Lord;

And shall make him of quick understanding in the fear of the Lord: and he shall not judge after the sight of his eyes, neither reprove after the hearing of his ears:" (Isaiah 11:2-3).

Heavenly Father, I appropriate this as a prayer for my children:

Father, I pray that the spirit of the Lord will rest upon my children: the spirit of wisdom and understanding, the spirit of counsel and might, the spirit of the knowledge and of the fear of the Lord.

Heavenly Father, I pray that you make my children of quick understanding in the fear of the Lord, that they will delight in the fear of the Lord, and they shall not judge after the sight of their eyes nor make decisions and judgements after what they hear but will have good spiritual discernment in Jesus' name. Amen.

33

GREAT SHALL BE THE PEACE OF MY CHILDREN

Father, your Word in the Book of Isaiah 54:13, *"All your children shall be taught by the Lord, And great shall be the peace of your children"*.

Father, l agree with your word that my children shall be taught of you, and they will walk in the paths of the Lord, in Jesus' name.

Great shall be the peace of my children, in Jesus' name. My children will bring me peace in Jesus' name. My children will also walk in the peace of the Lord in Jesus' name and bring peace to others in Jesus' name. Amen.

34

LORD, GIVE MY CHILDREN A HUNGER FOR YOUR WORD

Heavenly Father, a love for your word is a foundation for our Christian walk.

Your word says in 1 Peter 2:2:

"As newborn babes, desire the sincere milk of the word, that ye may grow thereby".

Father, l ask that you give my children a hunger for your word so that they grow in Christ, in Jesus' name.

As my children grow in you, they will move from milk to the strong meat of your word, in Jesus' name. Amen.

35

LORD, OPEN THEIR HEARTS TO YOUR WORD

Heavenly Father, your word says in the Book of Acts 16:14 (KJV):

"And a certain woman named Lydia, a seller of purple, of the city of Thyatira, which worshipped God, heard us: whose heart the Lord opened, that she attended unto the things which were spoken of Paul".

Lord, just as you opened Lydia's heart to your word, and she attended unto the things that were spoken, I pray that you open my children's hearts to your word.

May they be attentive, heed your word, and make it a priority in their lives, in Jesus' name. Amen.

36

EYES THAT SEE AND EARS THAT HEAR

Father, your word say in the Book of Proverbs 20:12:

"The hearing ear, and the seeing eye, the Lord hath made even both of them".

In the Book of Matthew 13:16, your word says, *"But blessed are your eyes for they see, and your ears for they hear".*

Father, I agree with your word that my children's eyes are opened to see and perceive the truth and that their ears hear the truth of your kingdom in Jesus' name. Amen.

37

LORD, TEACH MY CHILDREN THE PRINCIPLES OF WALKING IN DIVINE HEALTH

L ord, your word says in the Book of Hosea 4:6: *"My people are destroyed for lack of knowledge"*.

Father, your word is clear that you desire your children to walk in divine health (Isaiah 53:4-4; 1 Peter 2:24; Romans 8:11).

Therefore, I pray that my children will know your revelation that healing and divine health belong to them.

Death and life are in the power of the tongue (Proverbs 18:21). I declare divine health over my children. My children will walk in the life of God, in Jesus' name. I call my generation healthy, walking in divine health, in Jesus' name. Amen.

38

GOOD DISCERNMENT IN CHOOSING THEIR RELATIONSHIPS

F ather, your Word says in the Book of Romans 8:14:

"For as many as are led by the Spirit of God, they are the sons of God".

Father, l pray that my children will have good discernment in their relationships. They will know how much permission they should give people access to them.

They will know when a season of a relationship is over in their lives.

They will not wrongly discern people you have placed in their lives for a purpose.

They will exercise good spiritual discernment in relationships, in Jesus' name.

39

DECLARE PSALM 1:1-3 OVER THEM

Father, your word says in the Book of Psalm 1:1-3:

"Blessed *is* the manWho walks not in the counsel of the ungodly,Nor stands in the path of sinners,Nor sits in the seat of the scornful;But his delight *is* in the law of the Lord,And in His law he meditates day and night.He shall be like a treePlanted by the rivers of water,That brings forth its fruit in its season,Whose leaf also shall not wither;And whatever he does shall prosper."

Father, I declare that my children will delight themselves in the law of the Lord. I pray that they will know the importance of meditating on the word of God and make this a practice by your grace in Jesus' name.

I declare that my children will be like trees planted by the rivers of water that bring forth their fruits in season, and whatever they do shall align with your will and counsel. They shall prosper in Jesus' name. Amen.

40

RESTORATION OF LOST TIME AND YEARS

H eavenly Father, your word says in the Book of Joel 2:25:

"And I will restore to you the years that the locust hath eaten, the cankerworm, and the caterpiller, and the palmerworm, my great army which I sent among you".

Father, l pray that where my children have lost time and years and have had setbacks for whatever reason, in your mercy, time will be restored to them in Jesus' name.

Father, l pray for divine acceleration and full recovery of all they have lost in Jesus' name. Amen.

41

CHOOSE THEIR SPOUSES WISELY

F ather, your word says in the Book of Amos 3:3

"Can two walk together, except they be agreed".

Marriage is a covenant that has grave long-term implications.

Lord, only you know the heart of man, the challenges that await in future, giftings and callings, the destiny of individuals, and how a person can change in the future.

So, I ask that all my children be led by your Spirit on this matter, in Jesus' name.

They will make wise decisions and choose wisely only after your direction and wisdom, in Jesus' name. Amen.

My children will only marry those ordained for them by your divine hand in Jesus' name.

42

CAUSE THEM TO LIVE IN THE RIGHT PLACE

Heavenly Father, location is crucial as it determines a number of factors, including associations, spiritual atmospheres, neighbours, and what can influence young children.

In Scripture, we see where you directed people to go from one place to another.

Your word says in the Book of 1 John 5:14-15:

"And this is the confidence that we have in him, that, if we ask any thing according to his will, he heareth us:

And if we know that he hear us, whatsoever we ask, we know that
we have the petitions that we desired of him".

Father, l ask that you cause my children to make the right decisions regarding their location and where they will live in Jesus' name.

43

DECLARE 2 CORINTHIANS 2:15 OVER THEM

F ather, your word says in the Book of 2 Corinthians 2:15:

"For we are to God the fragrance of Christ among those who are being saved and among those who are perishing".

Father, I pray that my children will walk in alignment with your heart and will. I pray that they will be a fragrance of Christ wherever they go, in Jesus' name. Amen.

44

ONLY THE BLESSING WORKS IN THEIR LIVES

F ather, your word says in the Book of Genesis 22:18 and the Book of Galatians 3:13-14:

"In your seed all the nations of the earth shall be blessed, because you have obeyed My voice"

"Christ hath redeemed us from the curse of the law, being made a curse for us: for it is written, Cursed is every one that hangeth on a tree:

That the blessing of Abraham might come on the Gentiles through Jesus Christ; that we might receive the promise of the Spirit through faith".

Father, I agree with your word that my children are blessed because Abraham obeyed you. I also agree with your word that the blessing of Abraham comes unto my children through Jesus Christ in Jesus' name.

Father, I declare in Jesus' name that only the blessing works and speaks for my children. Amen.

45

DECLARE ISAIAH 54:17 OVER THEM

F ather, your word says in the Book of Isaiah 54:17:

"No weapon that is formed against thee shall prosper; and every tongue that shall rise against thee in judgment thou shalt condemn. This is the heritage of the servants of the Lord, and their righteousness is of me, saith the Lord".

Father, I declare in Jesus' name that no weapon in any way, formed or fashioned against my children, will prosper in Jesus' name.

Every tongue that rises against them I condemn in Jesus' name.

Father, I thank you that the righteousness of my children is of thee because they belong to you, know you, and have made Jesus Christ their righteousness.

46

BLESS YOUR GENERATIONS TO COME

J acob did not only bless Joseph (Genesis 48:15), but he blessed Joseph's children (Genesis 48:20).

The scriptures tell us that life and death are in the power of the tongue (Proverbs 18:21).

In your own words, begin to bless your generations to come, even your children's children.

Speak that they will know the Lord, be in health and prosperity, and God's favour to rest upon them. Bless them so they will fulfil their God-ordained destiny.

47

THAT THEY WILL GROW IN GRACE AND THE KNOWLEDGE OF OUR LORD

F ather, your word says in the Book of 2 Peter 3:18:

"but grow in the grace and knowledge of our Lord and Savior Jesus Christ".

Heavenly Father, I pray that my children will grow in grace and the knowledge of our Lord Jesus Christ, in Jesus' name.

Father, I pray that they will desire more of you, which will cause them to hunger and thirst for righteousness, which is one ingredient of growth in you, in Jesus' name. Amen.

48

LORD, HELP THEM TO APPLY THEIR HEARTS UNTO WISDOM

F ather, your word says in the Book of Psalm 90:12:

"So teach us to number our days, that we may apply our hearts unto wisdom".

Lord, l pray that you teach my children to number their days. Let them know that they will not always be young so that they can apply their hearts unto wisdom, in Jesus' name. Amen.

49

PRAY EPHESIANS 1:17-23 OVER THEM

Father, your word says in the Book of Ephesians 1:17-23 (KJV):

17 That the God of our Lord Jesus Christ, the Father of glory, may give unto you the spirit of wisdom and revelation in the knowledge of him:

18 The eyes of your understanding being enlightened; that ye may know what is the hope of his calling, and what the riches of the glory of his inheritance in the saints,

19 And what is the exceeding greatness of his power to us-ward who believe, according to the working of his mighty power,

20 *Which he wrought in Christ, when he raised him from the dead, and set him at his own right hand in the heavenly places,*

21 *Far above all principality, and power, and might, and dominion, and every name that is named, not only in this world, but also in that which is to come:*

22 *And hath put all things under his feet, and gave him to be the head over all things to the church,*

23 *Which is his body, the fulness of him that filleth all in all.*

Heavenly Father, I now personalise this prayer over my children:

That the God of our Lord Jesus Christ, the Father of glory, may give unto them the spirit of wisdom and revelation in the knowledge of Him:

That the eyes of their understanding being enlightened; that they may know what the hope of your calling is, and what the riches of the glory of your inheritance in the saints are,

And what is the exceeding greatness of Your power towards them that believe, according to the working of Your mighty power,

Which you wrought in Christ, when you raised Him from the dead and set Him at Your own right hand in the heavenly places,

Far above all principality, and power, and might, and dominion, and every name that is named, not only in this world, but also in that which is to come: And hath put all things under his feet, and gave him to be the head over all things to the church,

Which is His body, the fullness of Him that fills all in all, in Jesus' Name. Amen.

50

Pray Ephesians 3:14-21
Over Them

F ather, in the Book of Ephesians 3:14-21 (KJV), your word
says:

*⁴ For this cause I bow my knees unto the Father of our Lord Jesus
Christ,*

¹⁵ Of whom the whole family in heaven and earth is named,

*¹⁶ That he would grant you, according to the riches of his glory, to
be strengthened with might by his Spirit in the inner man;*

*¹⁷ That Christ may dwell in your hearts by faith; that ye, being
rooted and grounded in love,*

18 May be able to comprehend with all saints what is the breadth, and length, and depth, and height;

19 And to know the love of Christ, which passeth knowledge, that ye might be filled with all the fulness of God.

20 Now unto him that is able to do exceeding abundantly above all that we ask or think, according to the power that worketh in us,

21 Unto him be glory in the church by Christ Jesus throughout all ages, world without end. Amen.

Father, I personalise this prayer for my children:

I bow my knees unto the Father of our Lord Jesus Christ,

Of whom the whole family in heaven and earth is named,

That He would grant my children, according to the riches of His glory, to be strengthened with might by His Spirit in their inner man;

That Christ may dwell in their hearts by faith; that they, being rooted and grounded in love,

May be able to comprehend with all saints what is the breadth, and length, and depth, and height;

And to know the love of Christ, which passes knowledge, that they might be filled with all the fullness of God.

Now unto Him who can do exceeding abundantly above all that we ask or think, according to the power that works in us,

Unto Him be glory in the Church by Christ Jesus throughout all ages, world without end. In Jesus' name. Amen.

SALVATION PRAYER

Father God, I come to you in Jesus' name. I admit that I am a sinner, and I now receive the sacrifice that Jesus Christ paid for me.

I confess with my mouth the Lord Jesus, and I believe in my heart that God raised Him from the dead.

I now declare that Jesus Christ is my Lord and Saviour.

Thank you, Father, for saving me in Jesus' name.

I am now your child. Amen.

If you've said this prayer for the first time, send an email to Bisiwriter@gmail.com . Start reading your Bible and ask the Lord to guide you to a good church.

ABOUT THE AUTHOR

About the Author

Bisi Oladipupo has been a Christian for many years and lives in the United Kingdom with her family.

She has attended a few Bible colleges, and she has completed a diploma in Biblical Studies from a UK Bible college. She has also obtained an associate degree in Bible and Theology from a USA School of Ministry.

She is a teacher of God's Word, coordinates Bible studies, and a Christian fellowship.

Her author page is www.bisiwriter.com

Her blog website is www.inspiredwords.org

You can contact Bisi by email at bisiwriter@gmail.com

ALSO BY BISI

The Twelve Apostles of Jesus Christ: Lessons We Can Learn

The Lord's Cup in Communion: The Significance of taking the Lord's Supper

Different Ways to Receive Healing from Scripture and Walk in Health

Believing on The Name of Jesus Christ: What Every Believer Needs to Know

The Mind and Your Christian Walk: The Impact of the mind on our Christian walk

Relationship Skills in the Bible: Scriptural Principles of relating to others

Afterword

If you enjoyed this book, please take a few moments to write a review of it online at the store where it was purchased. Thank you

Printed in Great Britain
by Amazon

42883053R00057